Fixing My Fu**ed Up

A story of Self Help, Self-Care and staying "Sane-ish."

Christina Chadouin

Author: Christina Chadouin

Table of Content

Copyrights 5
Introduction 6
Growing up 8
Adulthood 13
Fixing Up 27
Traumas to overcome 29
   1. Hormone situation 30
   2. Anxiety 33
      What causes anxiety and depression? 40
   3. Depression 44
      Difference between the Anxiety and Depression 49
Things That Really Help Me Out! 51
   1- Journaling 53
   2- Fitness and Yoga 63
      Tip to Get Motivated 67
   3- Meditating 71
      Tips to make it Easier 74
      Five Mediational Techniques That Helped Me Out 76
   4- Breathing techniques to calm you down 77
   5- Try a new hobby 79

Author: Christina Chadouin

90 Days Challenge 88
Books I like 97
People to Thank 99

Copyrights

Wild Eagle Publishing

Copyright © Christy Chadouin

Wild Eagle logo is © 2020 Wild Eagle Publishing.

All rights reserved. No part of this book may be used in any form whatsoever without written permission of the author.

ISBN: 978-1-7345021-3-8 paperback

ISBN: 978-1-7345021-4-5 eBook

ISBN: 978-1-7345021-5-2 audiobook

All photos are from the author's private collection.

Author: Christina Chadouin

Introduction

"There are options in life."

The above statement can be hard to believe when life is hard on us. This book is sprinkled with thoughts and tips that will hopefully help some of you. Maybe something that I share will echo through your soul, or my experiences will help you understand you are not alone. Just knowing that others have had to dig deep inside themselves to determine what is important in life can be helpful.

I wanted to write this book to share my story with others in hopes of connecting. In this world that seems at times to get more angry, violent, and less compassionate, it's no wonder more, and more people are committing suicide, trying to escape reality with drugs or alcohol, etc. On a more positive note, luckily, more people are also getting help and seeking professional care as well! Which is wonderful! Mental health is important! It seems in the last few years, especially between Covid, entitlement, political wars; real wars, and mass shootings; life has been radical and insane! Which also helps make sense of why we all sometimes feel like we're going crazy trying to handle it all! We are in fight or flight mode all the time now! Then we

Author: Christina Chadouin

become desensitized to things that matter! I wanted to take a moment to share with you my story and thoughts. In addition, some of the things that have helped me feel more "sane-ish."

There are options. In addition, I hope to connect through my experience, something that may help you! At least give you a good read.

Author: Christina Chadouin

Growing up

Even as a child, I was a little fucked up. I didn't even nap as a baby, and to this day, I still can't nap. Part of that is, of course, insomnia. Sleep disorders tend to be genetic. I got insomnia from my dad, while my brother got sleep apnea from my mother. That's not the only thing you gain from your lineage. Even a lot of our 'brain issues' are passed down generation after generation. We have genetic stress from our ancestors.

I've always been a positive person and usually pretty happy! Although, I have always had dark thoughts and dreams that make people shake their heads. I've never been able to explain it, but that's just how my brain works.

When I was little, my mom used to tell me stories of how I would sleep walk with my eyes open, have a conversation with her, and then go to bed. As a teenager, I have called people and had conversations in my sleep. I've even changed clothes and gone back to bed! Luckily, I don't do that anymore. I'm guessing that stopped after maturing into an adult and maybe sleeping an hour or two more. In addition, thanks to yoga and other methods, I sleep way more now than I ever have in my entire life! Which is great considering I sleep six to eight hours now when I used to only sleep one to two hours.

Author: Christina Chadouin

I was born in Ohio; my mom was always present while my dad was in and out of our lives a lot. We didn't have money. A lot of the time, we lived either with my dad's parents, my mom's parents, or in an apartment or townhouse. Luckily, for me, we moved to Houston when I was eight. I'm very grateful to have grown up in a bigger city that gave me opportunities to explore different cultures. If you've never been to Houston, it's much more than cows and oil! Bigger municipalities have more things to do that include various groups of people, often from different cultures, which I found interesting and stimulating. Variety of languages, dialects, colors of skin, food aromas, and on and on sure made my growing-up years more thought provoking and fascinating. My mom always made sure that she found things to entertain us, even with little money. We went to the beach a lot. She would get us season passes to enjoy most of the summer at the amusement park. We would go on picnics and explore parks. In addition, since we usually lived in an apartment, there was always a swimming pool.

Author: Christina Chadouin

For most of my life, my dad has been a liar, cheater, and not the best person in general. However, he's also one of those people who are very charismatic and can make people love him no matter what. I will give him some credit, though; when he was around, he was a good dad. He helped me get my second car and taught me how to drive a stick shift.

Nevertheless, the constant in and out and lying, as well as cheating, has been going on since I was a child. It wears on your soul. There was an instance when I was less than five years old, but I still remember. While my mom was away, he drove me at night to his mistress house, thinking I was asleep. Then he left me in the car. Who leaves a five-year-old alone in a car at night? Unfortunately, for him, I have a very good memory and told my mother. I actually directed her there even though I was lying down in his lap the majority of the time. That's how she found out about that particular mistress.

He has gone as far as to lie to various family members about moving cars out of a rental agency he used to work for to sell them! The family thought they were helping but could have been arrested for doing something that was illegal. He has lied to priests about previous marriages, as well as his children, so he could get married again. The list goes on and on and on. During all of these lies, he continues to claim to be a devout Christian. This behavior

Author: Christina Chadouin

has influenced why I am not religious. I have seen too much hypocrisy in my life about Christianity and being a good human and then doing horrible things to people. Now I am not saying that Christianity is horrible. I know many wonderful humans that are Christian. I think we all need something to keep ourselves in check. But others use it to take advantage of people, which is very unfortunate.

I personally don't care what you study or believe as long as you are a good human and care for others. It's not that complicated. Just be kind! It's pretty sad that we have to go around putting it on bumper stickers and T-shirts to remind people to be nice to each other! However, hey, if it helps!

Oddly enough, I still talk to my dad. Even though I contemplate not doing it from time to time. We are not close, but I do get a five-minute phone call or text about two or three times a year from him, and I do the same. He still tries to get me to go to church. In addition, I tell him my church is outside in nature. He's pushed me a couple of times really close to telling him "Do you really want to compare notes on who the better human is?" He even screwed up his last marriage from one of the mistresses he had for 30 years and cheated on her too and in his 60s! Some people never learn their lessons. In addition, he didn't even tell me they got divorced. I had to find out from another relative. Why can't you just be honest? I wish him

Author: Christina Chadouin

well and care for him, but he's got a lot of karma to make up for.

Anyway, I am sharing this just to give you an idea of my childhood and background to my point of view. My mom was very loving and when my dad was around, he was actually a great dad. But my mom was there for me, always! She always encouraged us that we could be whatever we wanted. Her actions for herself didn't always show that, but I am grateful for this lesson she instilled in us. In fact, sometimes I was a little too much of her friend, instead of her daughter, confiding in me with her marriage issues. But I knew it came from her with love. She always did her best to make sure that my brother and I were taken care of. Unfortunately, she passed away eight years ago. She always took care of us and always showed us, love. We were poor but loved. I am forever grateful for that.

Author: Christina Chadouin

Adulthood

Due to seeing all of these lies and my view of marriage even as a child, I said I never wanted to get married. When I was 18, I was out of the house and living with my boyfriend at the time. My mom lived in a townhome and had a couple that moved in next door and wanted me to meet them. They were nice and close in age to my boyfriend and I. We used to go to parties, dance, and hang out together. Their marriage was shaky and then they moved to another place not far away.

We didn't see them as much and when I spoke with them again, they were getting a divorce. I was sorry to hear that but she seemed very jealous and even accused me of interfering. That was not the case at the time. However, he and I started talking more. I wasn't happy in my relationship either and was thinking of breaking up. The more we talked, the more it seemed we were very compatible and wanted the same things out of a relationship. We both did end our relationships and did start dating. It seemed amazing like soul mates! In addition, he proposed. When I finally met someone whom I thought was my soulmate, even then I was engaged for several years.

Author: Christina Chadouin

"To be sure". We did have a great marriage for a while. We had many common interests. We both loved motorcycles and riding, hiking, rock climbing, dancing, music, and so forth. We were both very outgoing. However, he being the same zodiac sign as my dad and even having a birthday one day apart, he started doing selfish things and did not think of the consequences of how it would affect both of us. I feel he always had this hungry ghost that he tried to fill with material items that just put us more and more in debt.

Author: Christina Chadouin

Do not get me wrong, I got on this journey with him as well. Then I realized how we were sinking ourselves. In addition, I did not want to be a part of it. Then he did the usual midlife crisis thing and had an affair with someone 13 years younger. She was also engaged. So quite the pick! We separated and I started dating. I warned him that she would cheat on him as well. Shocker! Not to give away the ending but obviously, she cheated on him. Guess who wanted to come back to Mama? He worked very hard to get me back, which I had never done. I always say there is a reason you break up with someone. So don't go back! But he did it! He worked his ass off and he got me back. It wasn't very long after that the trophy had been received and interest was lost again. I was starting to feel the same. So, I ended it. I told him then that I loved and cared for him, but neither one of us are happy and I don't see the point. Let's both move on with our lives and I will never come back to you. Little did I know, he was already starting to see someone else? I found out after I moved.

It was a long strung-out divorce that we had to file bankruptcy for due to debt. And even worse a foreclosure on the house we shared because I couldn't afford to keep it myself. Nobody put a gun to my head through all of this. In addition, I do take responsibility for my choices. However, sometimes you do things that are bad decisions

Author: Christina Chadouin

because you love someone. However, I don't want to play the victim here. I feel we grew further and further in different directions. He could be a wonderful person a lot of the time. When we separated, he did give me some money to help me get on my feet. I still feel he is a good person but needs to work on the inner peace he is lacking. I truly hope one day he finds it.

Author: Christina Chadouin

******

After a long-drawn-out divorce, I made the awful mistake of dating a narcissistic gas lighter. This was very new to me. I have never experienced anything like that before. It's wild how someone can turn things around and make you seem like the crazy one when they are manipulating the hell out of you! We weren't together very long. Less than a year. I made the mistake of moving in with him. Which lasted for about a month. My mom died right before Thanksgiving unexpectedly. He was there, seemed so supportive, and drove with me to help take care of all of the arrangements.

My brother had disappeared a couple of years prior. Moved to I have no idea where. And my only way to contact him was through Facebook messenger. When mom died, I had to message him to let him know. He would only reply on messenger. He wouldn't even call me. He wouldn't even come to see his mother who helped supply him with love and nurturing his whole life! I couldn't believe it. I couldn't believe he couldn't even have the decency to pick up the phone! In addition, see mom one last time before she was cremated. It broke my heart.

My mom didn't have any money nor did she have life insurance, so I had to cover the cost of that. She also was almost a hoarder. We had many things to get rid of and

Author: Christina Chadouin

donate in a short amount of time before I had to come back to work. I'm a hairstylist and Thanksgiving and Christmas are my busiest times. Literally, the day we came back, he (Jekyll and Hyde) started acting weird and acting like I was cheating on him. He would stalk me at work sometimes to make sure that I was there. Because you know, I had nothing else to do! WTF? I worked my ass off at work and was heading out to the car to call him and let him know I was on my way home. Little did I know he had already shown up at my job in the parking lot. He scared the shit out of me! When I asked, "What are you doing here," he says "what the fuck?" I say, "Excuse me?" He asked, "Why I hadn't called him yet," I said, "Because I just finished work! I am exhausted can we go home?" Once back home, he continued to push and push me until I almost jumped off the balcony of our apartment. Literally! My mom had just died a few days before and I was working my butt off and now this? Are you serious? After he realized how far he had pushed me, he changed the tune.

We had a "nice" Thanksgiving the next day and that weekend he completely lost his mind. We went to a bar to watch a football game he wanted to see. They had couches around a TV so it was community style. There was another person there talking to both of us. The guy went to the rest room and my gas lighter started accusing me of flirting with the guy! Also asked me who I was texting. I had

Author: Christina Chadouin

already shown him it was the woman I worked for because she was planning a trunk show at the salon. I couldn't believe it! We then left to drop me off at a nail appointment and I guess he went to a bar and drank. When he picked me up, he started calling me names and just saying awful things. When we got home, it blew up! He started chasing me around asking to look at my phone and I told him no. I had to call 911 as he was chasing me through the house and then he tried to pin me down. I had bruises on my hands and arms where he was trying to hold me down. The only thing that saved me was the 911 voice that came through on the other side of the phone.

He got up off me and started throwing my stuff into the hallway of our high-rise. I had to grab my dogs because I was scared he would do something to them. So then, we (the dogs and I) were sitting out in the hallway, waiting for the police to arrive. When they finally showed up, he answers the door and says I don't live there! And tells them he just found out I was cheating on him and that's why he was upset. I lost my shit! I said if I don't live here why do you have all of my clothes and furniture in your house, my dog's bowls on the floor, and my mother's ashes that just arrived through the mail to this address? The police knew then I was telling the truth and made him let us in so I could get my things. I was so stressed out that I just grabbed some clothes and my dogs and took them off to a

Author: Christina Chadouin

friend's house. I also had to work the next day. My friend watched my dogs, and I went to work and tried to figure out how I was going to get my life back together.

I had done it. I was homeless and had hit rock bottom. I immediately got sick because I was so stressed.

I feel like in situations like these when you have one trauma after another your brain just says "OK enough! We are shutting this shit down because we can't handle it anymore!

******

"Survival mode! I did not have time to grieve my mother, I had to find a place to live and figure out how I was going to survive! As fucked up as our brains are sometimes, they really do try to help us. I put a restraining order on him. I told one of my good friends about the situation that just happened the night before.

This is where things turn around and become crazy good! Well, not immediately, but it leads to better things. I'm explaining to my friend how I am now broke paying for my mother's funeral expenses and paying rent in a place where I now no longer live, and I am homeless. I needed someone to help me get my things under a police escort to make sure the narcissistic gas lighter didn't do something crazy again. She tells me that she has a friend that just moved back into town and is always willing to help anyone

Author: Christina Chadouin

in need. He has a truck and a trailer so I know he can help you move your things. My first thought was "if he just moved here, isn't he busy getting his own life together? " She said I'm going to call him; I know he will help. Sure enough, he did. Now obviously I was not looking for anyone or for a relationship whatsoever!

This poor man shows up with my friend and the police that he didn't even know about, because she didn't tell him, to help some stranger move out of a crazy man's house and into a storage unit until I can find a place to live. One of my other friends offered for me and my dogs to stay with her until I found something. Which I was so very grateful for. Not only did he help me move, but this wonderful man had to come to the storage facility again the next day because it was already closed by the time we were done moving. Therefore, he helped me move all of my things into a storage facility and would not accept a single penny to help. I told him to please keep my number and if he ever needs anything to please, please, please, let me know. I offered to give him free haircuts forever, lol. He said he has helped many damsels in distress. I told him I'm not usually a damsel in distress and you've caught me at my worst possible time.

Since that awful experience was new to me, I wanted to understand how to avoid this type of person again! I had a couple of other friends who also went through a very

Author: Christina Chadouin

similar experience. One was worse! They gave me a couple of books to read. I started diving in! I did not ever want to be in this situation again and wanted to educate myself on how to avoid it. I have to say, I had to apologize for my perspective on this prior to this incident. I would see people stay in abusive relationships and say why don't you leave? But sometimes they make you feel like you're the bad guy! Or they leave you feeling too scared to leave because of what they might do. In addition, I didn't realize that before. I also feel I needed to go through that experience for that reason as well. So I would be more understanding of others in that kind of situation.

A few weeks later, I found a place to live and moved in with the help of friends. The wonderful man that helped me and I stayed in touch texting here and there. He was traveling for work at the time. During that time, I had a dream with my mom in it. In the dream, I was introducing her to my new wonderful man. I could not see his face but in the dream, his name was Jay. She went on and on about how happy she was I was with him and what a great man he was.

A few weeks after that, Mr. Sweetheart finally took me up on letting me cut his hair but only if he buys me dinner afterward. I was like "oh! He does like me!" We had a wonderful dinner after the haircut and actually closed the place down because we were talking so much! We had a

Author: Christina Chadouin

wonderful make-out session, and I really liked him! It was a few dates later that I found out that sometimes he goes by Jay for short. I was like "what?!?!" I knew then he was the guy in my dreams with my mom! And I knew then why I had to go through the horrible experience with the other man who attacked me because otherwise, I would've never met this man any other way! There is a silver lining! It's been eight years now and we are still together, very happily! I still call him my knight in shining armor because he saved me!

Don't get me wrong, we have a few arguments just like anybody does. But we love and respect each other and have very great communication! Don't settle! Learn from your experiences what you don't want and what you do want. And wait till you find it! No one is perfect. But you have to find the person that works for you. And along the way, you can enjoy your awesome self! Sometimes, you need that time to figure yourself out. Enjoy yourself! You are the only person that is with you for your entire life! You might want to learn to like yourself and be good friends with yourself! This is going to be one of those times where I say the cheesy thing about things happening for a reason and bad situations teaching you what you don't want later in your life. I do believe that! I lived it and learned from it.

******

Author: Christina Chadouin

So now, you get the basis of my relationships and me with men. I won't even go into my brother. Let's just say it's not good. I wish him well also. Along the journey, though I have met wonderful people and I've met total assholes, just like the rest of us! Life is messy, fucked up, and complicated sometimes. But it can also be amazing, beautiful, and so loving! I have done many things in my life. I have always had an adventurous spirit! Some of my family thinks I'm insane or a lesbian or both. Among other opinions. Just because I like to go to pride festivals and I have many gay friends. Alternatively, I travel to different countries by myself. We love each other, my family and I but have very different outlooks on life. And that's ok! I don't really care. It's my life and I need to live it the way I want to! As should they. I feel like you should always care for others but don't let other people's thoughts and opinions stop you from what you really want to do and be! Most people on their deathbed's biggest regret is not living the life they wanted to because they were too busy pleasing others. Don't be that person!

I have raced motorcycles. I have rock climbed. I have backpacked several hundred miles in distant and some foreign lands all by myself. I have started multiple businesses. I am very independent and I always like to try new things. As long as it doesn't hurt others, I am pretty

Author: Christina Chadouin

game. All in all, I feel like I've had a very good life. But even in some of the best moments, I have had dark thoughts.

When I was a teenager, I went into Goth mode for a while before it was even Goth. Learned about witchcraft, tried drugs, and snuck into clubs I wasn't old enough to be in. I loved to party! And being an insomniac, was quite beneficial. I could get two hours of sleep on average and still make A's as an honors student. I would sneak out all the time to go dancing or get in trouble.

I am so grateful my mom didn't know half of the things that I did growing up or she would've died earlier. Thank goodness, Facebook was not out then! All of those pictures and evidence, no thank you! But I used to cut on myself and have suicidal thoughts even then. In addition, in my best times, sometimes that still doesn't leave.

I've always been an extrovert. Always been a people person. A social butterfly. I've always enjoyed meeting new people and going to new places. Every job I've ever had has been some kind of service job. I've waited tables, I've been a bartender, and taught aerobics, step, and Yoga. I put myself through cosmetology school, while still doing bookkeeping for a lady I worked for in high school, and I bartended at night after school. My need for little sleep really kicked in during this time. I'm so grateful for it!

Author: Christina Chadouin

I've always liked doing more than 1 thing. After becoming a hairstylist, I still taught yoga for quite a while. Now, I am still a hairstylist and I run two online businesses. Moreover, I trade stocks. As much as I love people I have to say, sometimes I want to smack them! I've definitely been jaded over the years but I try to remember there are a lot of great people out there. I definitely need some of my own private time to recharge my batteries to be ready for the next social event. I work 40 minutes from home and I like the quiet time there and back. That's my recharging time. It definitely helps.

Author: Christina Chadouin

Fixing Up

Life is messy. Humans are not supposed to be perfect and nor are we! So stop trying to be perfect if that's your gig. We have emotions, feelings, and thoughts, and none of it is perfect and sometimes makes no sense. But that's OK. Our crazy human lives on this earth are not supposed to be picture-perfect. We are supposed to be messy and make mistakes. That's how we get better! We should reflect and grow through our experiences; good and bad ones. Showing that you're vulnerable doesn't mean you are weak, it actually shows courage to show that you have the rawness and vulnerability that you should have as a human.

We should care about each other. I know some people make you want to punch them in the face. They are a little harder. But we should still care! It doesn't mean we can change the assholes, but maybe we can avoid them more and send them good vibes. Always try to surround yourself with the people who truly support you and that are kind. It definitely helps! And don't forget to pass on that kindness to others who need your support! You never know what someone is going through.

Author: Christina Chadouin

I just want you to know we are all messy and have our issues whether we are willing to admit it or not. However, that's life as a human. If it were supposed to be easy, we wouldn't have hate, war, death, and sickness. These are all things that we have to face and it's not pretty! Show kindness to yourself and others for our messiness.

Author: Christina Chadouin

Traumas to overcome

We have all been through many different things in our lives. Like most women, I have been sexually harassed, sexually abused, mentally abused, physically abused, and emotionally abused. Now I'm not saying that women are the only ones that go through this. But let's be honest, the odds are much higher. And I'm not saying I have been in your shoes. And I know some people that have been through way, way, way more bad shit than I have! And still turned out to be some of the happiest, most positive people I have ever met! My point is we all have had traumas, trials, and tribulations. And if you can just take a moment to realize your self-worth, then you can move forward. Emotions only last for 90 seconds unless you create an entire feeling out of it. Next time you get all worked up, remind yourself of this. Take a few breaths and ask yourself after 90 seconds, "is it as serious as I think? Is there something I can do about it? If there isn't, then there's no need to continue, and just do your best to Move On. I know this is way easier said than done! I have to remind myself of this very often!

Author: Christina Chadouin

1. Hormone situation

I have a pretty healthy body. I do my best to take care of it. Not to say that I don't enjoy my wine, a margarita, or junk food from time to time. But for the most part, I try to stay healthy. I take supplements; cook healthy most of the time. Blah blah blah.

However, in the past couple of years, I started to see big changes in my behavior. Even if I was in a spot where I felt my life was fantastic, I still felt suicidal and hopeless. I have a friend and some clients that are psychiatrists, psychologists, and psych nurses. I thought maybe I was becoming premenopausal and that it was screwing up my behavior. So first I tried natural supplements and did my usual go-to's. Yoga, hiking, camping, journaling. The usual things that get me back on track.

Then I thought, maybe once I get on vacation it'll be better. My man and I went on a wonderful trip to Costa Rica for two weeks. We had a wonderful time! However, even as I was thinking of coming back, I started deteriorating. By the time I came back, I was seriously contemplating suicide. In addition, all I could think was what is wrong with me? I know I have a good life! I know I am so grateful for my health and everything else! Why do I feel like this? I felt like I was losing my damn mind! WTF!? I finally spoke to my friend in therapy and told her I do not want to

Author: Christina Chadouin

live and I don't know why. I need help! I know I should not feel like this! She went on to explain to me that she has several clients going through this phase of life that start to feel like this or become very aggressive or violent. Hormones! I told her that I had already tried all the usual things that make me better and nothing was working! She suggested that I go on a small dose of Zoloft.

Now I am not a big fan of meds. Many times, I feel like the symptoms they give you are worse than what you're taking it for! But she knows me and she also knows how sensitive my body can be to meds in general. A lot of the time, things that affect other people do the opposite on me. It wasn't any different this time at first. She put me on a very small dose because she knows that things hit me hard. She also told me that I might want to take it at night because it tends to make people feel sleepy at first. Of course, for me, I didn't sleep for three days. Which was the amount of time that I took it. I stopped for a couple of days and I was going to try something else. But during those two days of not taking it, it was surprising to see how much more triggered and reactive I was! I was shocked! I was like holy shit!

I really need this stuff! So, I did the opposite. Instead of taking it at night, I started taking it in the morning and it totally worked! I felt normal again! Whatever that is! I always tease that that's just the setting on a washing machine. But I felt like myself! I actually felt happy and

Author: Christina Chadouin

didn't feel like I was just gonna blow up every time something triggered me. It was wonderful! I've heard lots of weird symptoms from some people. And we all respond to things very differently.

As I just explained. There are a lot of bad raps that antidepressants and meds do to people. And I'm not saying it's not true. But some people do need it! I did! I am now on half of the dose I was on before which is barely anything. But I feel at the moment it's still what I need to keep in check. I don't think I will need it forever but even if I do, if it helps...

Sometimes it can just be a couple of supplements that get you back in place! Or a 20-minute walk every day. Or going and petting a dog for 15 minutes. If you're not sure what to do, just try something. Give it a shot. You don't know until you try to help yourself. You're not alone. I know it feels like that sometimes but you're not. I care for you and I want you to succeed in life. I want you to be happy. There's so much crazy shit going on in this world right now we need to help each other! And I hope something in this book helps you!

Author: Christina Chadouin

One of the books I read recently that I feel explains the scientific part of why we feel so wrecked but does it in layman's terms is Unfuck your brain by Faith G Harper.

If you're interested, I will have a list of other books that I feel are worth a go.

2. Anxiety

I was in anxiety for several months, until I decided to get help. What helped me was therapy, medication, and a support system. If you're struggling with anxiety, please don't be afraid to seek help!

There are different types of anxieties and different treatments.

Author: Christina Chadouin

Anxiety disorders come in many different forms, such as social anxiety, phobias, panic disorder, and generalized anxiety disorder. The best way to treat anxiety is to talk to a doctor or mental health professional. They can help you figure out what type of anxiety you have and the best way to treat it. There are also many helpful self-care techniques that can lessen the symptoms of anxiety.

Let us discuss different forms of anxiety to help you better understand your condition:

    a. Obsessive-compulsive disorder
    b. Panic disorder
    c. Post-traumatic disorder
    d. Social anxiety disorder
    e. Specific phobia

Panic disorder is characterized by recurrent, unexpected panic attacks. A panic attack is a period of intense fear or discomfort that comes on suddenly and peaks within minutes. During a panic attack, you may experience heart palpitations, chest pain, shortness of breath, dizziness, or abdominal distress. Panic attacks can occur at any time, even during sleep. People with panic disorder often live in fear of another attack and may avoid places where an attack has occurred in the past. They may also avoid activities or situations that they believe might trigger an attack. Panic disorder is treated with medication, therapy, or a combination of both.

Author: Christina Chadouin

Medications used to treat the panic disorder include antidepressants, beta-blockers, and anti-anxiety medications. Therapy for panic disorder can include cognitive-behavioral therapy (CBT), exposure therapy, and relaxation techniques.

Social anxiety disorder (SAD) is characterized by intense fear or anxiety about social situations, such as meeting new people, public speaking, or going to parties. People with SAD often worry that they will be judged by others or embarrassed in public. They may avoid social situations altogether or endure them with great discomfort. SAD is treated with medication, therapy, or a combination of both. Medications used to treat SAD include antidepressants, beta-blockers, and anti-anxiety medications. Therapy for SAD can include CBT, exposure therapy, and relaxation techniques.

Obsessive-compulsive disorder (OCD) is characterized by intrusive, unwanted thoughts (obsessions) and repetitive behaviors (compulsions) that are time-consuming and cause distress or interfere with daily life. OCD is treated with medication, therapy, or a combination of both. Medications used to treat OCD include antidepressants, anti-anxiety medications, and antipsychotic medications. Therapy for OCD can include CBT, exposure therapy, and mindfulness-based stress reduction.

Author: Christina Chadouin

Post-traumatic stress disorder (PTSD) is characterized by intrusive, distressing memories of a traumatic event, such as a natural disaster, military combat, or sexual assault. People with PTSD may also experience flashbacks, nightmares, and avoidance of places or situations that remind them of the trauma. PTSD is treated with medication, therapy, or a combination of both. Medications used to treat PTSD include antidepressants, anti-anxiety medications, and antipsychotic medications. Therapy for PTSD can include CBT, exposure therapy, and eye movement desensitization and reprocess (EMDR).

A specific phobia is an intense fear of a specific object or situation, such as heights, animals, or flying. People with a specific phobia will go to great lengths to avoid the object or situation. Specific phobias are treated with exposure therapy, which gradually exposes the person to the feared object or situation in a safe and controlled setting. Anxiety is a normal reaction to stress and can be helpful in some situations. However, when anxiety is constant or overwhelming, it can be disabling. There are many different types of anxiety disorders, each with its own symptoms and treatment options. If you are experiencing symptoms of anxiety, talk to your doctor or a mental health professional for diagnosis and treatment.

Author: Christina Chadouin

I have been through challenges when it comes to mental health. I have experienced anxiety and depression. I have been on medication, and in therapy, and have done everything in my power to try to get better. Some days are good, and some days are bad. But I am still here, fighting the good fight.

If you are struggling with mental health, know that you are not alone. There are millions of people just like you who are fighting the same battle. You are not weak or crazy. You are strong and brave. In addition, you can get through this.

I am not leaving you alone here; I have learned many things through my own journey that I want to share with you. Here are some things that have helped my mental health.

1. Reach out for help - Don't be afraid to ask for help from family, friends, or a professional. It takes a lot of courage to admit that you need help, but it is so worth it. There are people who care about you and want to help you get better.

2. Medication - Medication can be a great tool in treating mental illness. It can help to stabilize moods, reduce anxiety, and improve sleep. If you are considering medication, talk to your doctor about what options are available to you.

Author: Christina Chadouin

3. Therapy - Therapy is another great treatment option for mental illness. It can help you understand your thoughts and feelings, work through your problems, and develop coping skills. If you are considering therapy, talk to your doctor or mental health professional about what options are available to you.

4. Exercise - Exercise is a great way to relieve stress and improve your mood. It can also help to increase energy levels and improve sleep.

5. Eat a healthy diet - Eating a healthy diet can help to improve your mood and energy levels. It is also important to drink plenty of water and avoid too much caffeine and alcohol.

6. Get enough sleep - Sleep is essential for good mental health. Aim for 7-8 hours of sleep every night. With insomnia, I still struggle sometimes with sleep but it has gotten so much better.

7. Avoid drugs and alcohol – If you are suffering, drugs and alcohol can make mental illness worse. If you are struggling with addiction, get help from a professional. Note: I know certain drugs and herbal remedies have also helped people overcome addictions and certain mental health issues. For instance, CBD has helped thousands of people with many physical and mental illnesses. I take a THC 10 mg edible on some nights to help with sleep. Of course, this is legal where I live. I don't smoke marijuana and only use the edibles to help me sleep sometimes. But it has helped others. Also, more therapists are getting into psilocybin therapy and ketamine therapy. Psilocybin therapy is an approach being investigated for mental health challenges. It combines the pharmacological effects of psilocybin, a psychoactive substance, with psychological support. And of course, you have heard of ayahuasca Shamen treatments. I personally know someone who was addicted to heroin and after her ayahuasca treatment, she never touched it again. I have heard many stories of how it has changed lives in a positive way. I have never experienced treatment myself (or heroin for that matter) but I'm happy to know of these alternatives that are helpful to some. But I would definitely recommend seeking professional therapists who practice these treatments for your own help.

8. Connect with others - Social support is vital for good mental health. Connect with family and friends, join a support group or volunteer in your community.

9. Take care of yourself - Be sure to take time for yourself and do things that make you happy. Relaxation techniques such as yoga, meditation, and aromatherapy can also help to reduce stress and improve your mood.

10. Seek professional help - If you are struggling with mental illness, seek professional help. There is no shame

Author: Christina Chadouin

in getting help from a doctor or therapist. Mental illness is a real and serious problem, but it is treatable. Don't hesitate to get the help you need.

What causes anxiety and depression?

As most women have, I have been sexually assaulted, sexually harassed, mentally abused, physically beaten up, and emotionally maltreated. I have been through some really tough times in my life. But, I am not Unique. Many other women have experienced the same things I have experienced.

There are a variety of different factors that can contribute to anxiety and depression. Some of the more common causes include:

- A family history of anxiety or depression
- Stressful life events, such as divorce, job loss, or the death of a loved one
- Traumatic experiences, such as abuse, sexual assault, or witnessing violence
- Health problems, such as thyroid disorders, heart disease, or chronic pain
- Certain medications, such as steroids or beta-blockers
- Substance abuse

Some major life events can trigger anxiety and depression. These include:

Author: Christina Chadouin

- Pregnancy and childbirth
- The death of a loved one
- A divorce or relationship problems
- A job loss or financial problems
- Moving to a new home
- Starting a new job or going back to school

Anxiety and depression are also sometimes caused by medical conditions. These include:

- Thyroid disorders
- Heart disease
- Cancer
- Chronic pain
- Asthma
- Gastrointestinal disorders
- Sleep apnea

In some cases, anxiety and depression can be caused by medications. These include:

- Steroids
- Beta-blockers
- Some antidepressants
- Some blood pressure medications

Substance abuse is another common cause of anxiety and depression. Substance abuse includes the use of alcohol, illegal drugs, and prescription medications.

Some of the more commonly abused substances include:

Author: Christina Chadouin

- Alcohol
- Cocaine
- Heroin
- Marijuana
- Methamphetamine

We have gone through these things in our life and I am going to discuss some of the important factors in detail.

1. Not getting enough sleep - Sadly, both adults and teenagers struggle with this issue. Due to the busy schedules of academics, extracurricular, family time, and (hopefully) some rest each day, kids frequently get less sleep than they need. In addition to making someone feel sleepy, not getting enough sleep can also make them exceedingly uncoordinated, and irritable, and have other negative effects.

2. High Expectations - Due to their high expectations of themselves, students today face a lot of stress. Not only that, but they also want to live up to and not disappoint their parents' expectations. The majority of teens aspire to achieve academic success in order to gain admission to Ivy League universities. Many kids balance part-time jobs and participation in after-school sports. Along with doing work around the house and participating in community events, they also wish to keep up their social lives. With such a busy schedule, they are not only exhausted but also have little time for relaxing, alone time, or even sleeping. Lack

Author: Christina Chadouin

of sleep makes anxiety worse, which makes for a vicious cycle that students find nearly impossible to break. Anxiety rises with sleep deprivation.

3. Financial pressure - As I stated earlier, in my childhood and some of my adult life we lacked money. I and my brother really had to help my mother when it came to expenses and whatnot, so we started working at a young age. From then on, I was constantly under pressure, the need to work more hours, get more money, help out with family expenses, and also deal with my own academics. This financial pressure leaves little room for anything else and can be a significant source of anxiety.

4. Relationship Problems - Whether it is a romantic relationship or a friendship, every teenager has experienced some kind of problem in their social life. These problems usually arise from misunderstandings or miscommunication between people. Some examples of relationship problems that can lead to anxiety are: being cheated on, being ghosted, having fights with friends, or feeling left out. All these problems can be very stressful and lead to anxiety.

5. Body Image Issues - One of the main sources of anxiety for teenagers is body image issues. In a society that constantly bombards us with images of "perfect" bodies, it's no wonder that so many teens struggle with their self-image. Teens compare themselves to these images and

Author: Christina Chadouin

often feel inadequate or like they don't measure up. This can lead to low self-esteem, depression, and anxiety.

6. Academic Pressure - I was good at academics, and I always strived to get good grades. However, the pressure to perform well academically is immense. The competition is tough, and the expectations are high. This pressure can lead to anxiety and stress.

7. Family Problems - Another common source of anxiety for teenagers is family problems. These can include divorce, fighting between parents, or even just having strict parents. Family problems can be very stressful and lead to anxiety.

8. Pressure to Fit In - In today's society, there is a lot of pressure to fit in. Teens feel like they have to conform to certain standards in order to be accepted by their peers. This pressure can lead to anxiety and stress.

3. Depression

Depression simply consumes you from the inside out. It takes control of you mentally, like a monster. The saddest part is that even though my family and friends were doing everything they could, I still felt at times alone. I was able to make anything stated to me into something negative. My worst opponent was actually me. Luckily I really didn't experience depression so much till I had hormone issues.

Author: Christina Chadouin

And when all the techniques I would usually do didn't work, I knew I needed assistance.

I feared that I had lost my identity and would never be the same. And when something would move me further from my goals, it would devastate me. I would be even angrier with myself to try harder. I wanted to be better. So I got the help I needed as I explained before.

The most terrifying aspect of my entire rehabilitation process is that I am the only one who can actually assist me. I've learned to alter my thought patterns and stop bullying myself; it's been challenging to break the habit, but I can see that I've changed for the better.

Undoubtedly, for all of us, the last couple of years has been a rollercoaster ride. I feel sometimes like I've gone through hell and back, but would I change my experiences? I don't think I would if I were to be completely honest. That doesn't mean depression is a good thing because it most certainly isn't, but I think you should try to make the best of your bad experiences.

The lesson that happiness is the most important thing in life would not have been learned if I hadn't gone through these experiences. You got to have the sweet and the sour. You don't appreciate the sweet as much until you have experienced the sour.

Author: Christina Chadouin

To those who are struggling, my one piece of advice would be to not suffer in quiet. There are individuals who have gone through and recovered from all that you are going through. Actually, their life experiences have shaped who they are today. You may think it's impossible to overcome, but have faith—you will.

Because depression is a disease like any other and is no more selfish than having a broken limb, you shouldn't feel bad about how you're feeling. The advice to treat yourself with the same decency and consideration as I would treat others has always been given to me. Why can't we be as understanding about our minds failing as we are of other body parts?

I have learned many things in my past years, and I continue to learn more about myself every day. Living with bouts of depression has been the hardest thing I have ever done, but also the most rewarding.

I want to share the different things that I have tried and what works for me, in hopes that it will assist somebody else who is struggling.

I have found that therapy, medication, and a support system are essential for my mental health. I started seeing a therapist when I lost my mom struggling with anxiety. Then again to help my hormone situation. Therapy has helped me to understand my

Author: Christina Chadouin

thoughts and emotions, and to develop coping mechanisms for when I'm feeling overwhelmed. In addition, I've found that medication can be helpful in managing the symptoms of my hormone issue. I've also been lucky to have a supportive family and group of friends who have always been there for me. Knowing that I have people who care about me and want to help me through tough times has been invaluable. Having these three things along with my own self-help and self-care has made a huge difference in my mental health.

I have also learned to be more understanding and accepting of myself. One of the most important things I have learned in life is to be more understanding and accepting of myself. We are all imperfect beings, and it is important to remember that no one is perfect. We all make mistakes, and we all have our own unique set of flaws. What matters is not that we are perfect, but that we are willing to learn from our mistakes and grow as people. I have also learned that it is okay to be different. We all have our own unique talents and gifts, and we should celebrate our differences instead of trying to conform to someone else's standards. By being more understanding and accepting of myself, I have become a happier and more well-rounded person.

It is important for me to pursue things that make me happy. Being happy is important to me for many

Author: Christina Chadouin

reasons. When I am happy, I am more productive, creative, and successful. I am also more likely to be healthy, both physically and mentally. Pursuing things that make me happy helps me to lead a more fulfilling life. It also allows me to be a better person, both to myself and to those around me. Of course, there are times when pursuing happiness can be difficult. But the effort is always worth it in the end. After all, as the saying goes, "Happiness is a journey, not a destination." And I am determined to enjoy the ride.

I think it is helpful to talk about my experiences. As a hairstylist, I have a lot of "therapy sessions" FOR my clients. And I am always honored and humbled to get to share such intimate moments with them of their thoughts, feelings, and life circumstances. And to a certain degree, we have both shared our life experiences. But I also want their time to be about them. And I love that about my job! I have always been one to share my thoughts and feel you always need to speak your mind. So I have always encouraged that with everyone. It helps in so many ways. Including making you feel less alone. In fact, talking about my depression has been one of the most helpful things I've done. It's helped me to connect with other people who have similar experiences, and it's given me a better understanding of my own condition. So if you're struggling with depression, I encourage you to find someone to talk to. You might be surprised at how much it helps.

Finally, I think it is possible for anyone to overcome depression. Depression is a serious mental illness that can have a profound effect on every aspect of a person's life. It can cause feelings of hopelessness and despair, leading sufferers to believe that things will never get better. However, I believe that it is possible for anyone to overcome depression. With the right treatment and support, anyone can learn to manage their symptoms and lead a fulfilling life. The first step is to reach out for help. If you or someone you know is struggling with depression, please don't hesitate to seek professional assistance. With the right help, anything is possible.

Difference between the Anxiety and Depression

It is very important to understand this difference as I was once very confused about it. Anxiety and Depression are two different things. Anxiety is the feeling of being worried, nervous, or afraid about something. Depression is a feeling of sadness, helplessness, and worthlessness. They are both mental disorders but anxiety is more common than depression.

Anxiety disorders can make you feel tense and irritable and can cause you to avoid things that you enjoy. Panic

Author: Christina Chadouin

attacks are also a symptom of anxiety disorders. Depression can make you feel sad all the time, have trouble sleeping, and lose interest in activities that you once enjoyed. It can be hard to concentrate and make decisions when you are depressed.

The main difference between anxiety and depression is that anxiety is more of a reaction to stress while depression is more of a reaction to life. Both disorders can be treated with medication and therapy. If you think that you might have either disorder, it is important to see a mental health professional for an evaluation.

Both anxiety and depression are serious mental disorders that can have a negative impact on your life. It is important to seek help from a mental health professional if you think you might be suffering from either disorder.

I have been through depression as well as anxiety and I can tell you that they are both serious disorders that need to be treated. If you think, you might have either disorder, follow all the possible solutions like medication, therapy, and even a change in lifestyle. Most importantly, never give up and keep fighting!

Author: Christina Chadouin

Things That Really Help Me Out!

I have always been an advocate for self-help. Being the independent person I am, I always felt like I could fix everything myself. Not the case. But I try. If I start feeling really down and miserable, I journal to get my feelings out. I used to backpack everywhere by myself, to be alone with no distractions from the internet or phone or anything. Just nature, my journal, and me. When I came back every time, I felt so much clearer and more confident about what I needed to do next. Nature is our connection. We have gotten so involved in tech, social media, TV, news, blah, blah, blah, that it has distracted us from our connection.

First don't watch the news often, if at all! It is purposely made to scare you and induce fear! All but 2% when a dog finds a home is bad news! That's how it sells! Give yourself a break from that negativity! Go outside on a beautiful day! See the blue skies and feel the sunshine warming your face. Listen to the birds! Feel the grass beneath your feet. See the beautiful flowers growing! See how amazing it is that all those little leaves on the trees grow back every year! Nature is amazing! And it can help you feel better!

Author: Christina Chadouin

I like to garden for many reasons, also because I am creating life and nurturing things to bloom and blossom. I like to get my hands in the dirt and see the worms aerating my soil for me to help my vegetables grow. Make connections. Feel the ground and touch the leaves and flowers. Go to a botanic garden and see all the amazing species of life around you.

Don't like people? I get it. Go volunteer at an animal shelter and help those little babies! When you focus on helping others, it distracts you from soaking in your own misery.

Don't believe me? Go to a coffee shop and buy the person behind you that coffee. See the change that you made in them, and how that makes you feel. Volunteering at an animal shelter and helping those poor animals find homes and get love. I know sometimes it feels like the last thing you want to do is help somebody else when you are the one that is suffering! It feels overwhelming! But it does help. Just try it!

I have my stories and learning linked to every part of my self-help journey and I am going to guide you on how self-help has helped me.

Let us start with journaling.

Author: Christina Chadouin

1- Journaling

I would love to tell you that I journal every day but that is not so. But I definitely have found in especially times of worry or trauma, to get things out on paper always feels better. That is not the only time I journal. I used a journal mostly when I went backpacking or camping. I still do that. But it's always good to get your thoughts out on paper. There is something about it that helps relieve the anxiety inside. Another thing that I have started journaling about is the things that I am grateful for. This can help transform your attitude and perspective as well. Damn, just living! How about that? The fact that we don't have to think to remember to breathe and have a heartbeat is amazing! Or maybe you just enjoyed your cup of tea or a good cup of coffee. If you have a roof over your head, have been fed today, and can read this, you are way, way, way ahead of many, many others on this earth! So just keep those things in mind when you can't seem to think of anything to be grateful for.

I am going to guide you in detail about journaling because it really helped me out and it will definitely help you too.

Journaling is the practice of writing down your innermost feelings, ideas, insights, and more. It can be typed, written, or illustrated. Both paper and a computer can be used. It's an easy, inexpensive method of enhancing your mental well-being.

Author: Christina Chadouin

Starting a journal is challenging. Writing every day can seem like labor, and for some individuals, that may be a turnoff. But even if you don't journal every day, its benefits might still be felt.

What Benefits Does Journaling Have to Your Mental Health?

When you express yourself artistically, such as when you write in a diary, you can focus on the aspects of your life that don't serve you and reduce stress. A notebook can be used to cultivate good habits, set and achieve objectives, manage your mental health, and alleviate worry, stress, and sadness. Your mental health can be significantly improved by investing even a small amount of time each day.

Benefits of Journaling

Journaling can be very beneficial for dealing with anxiety, illness, burnout at work, or any other type of stress. Moreover;

It can speed up physical healing. Physical health may be affected by journaling. According to a study conducted on 49 persons in New Zealand, those who spent 20 minutes writing about their emotions related to traumatic situations recovered more quickly after a biopsy than those who wrote about their usual activities. In a similar vein, sick days among college students were lower among

Author: Christina Chadouin

those who wrote about stressful occurrences as opposed to those who wrote about uninteresting subjects like their rooms.

It helps with brooding. Writing about a difficult experience might help you stop obsessively pondering and ruminating about what happened, but the timing is crucial. According to some studies, writing about a terrible occurrence right away can make you feel worse.

It creates awareness. You can have a better understanding of a challenging circumstance by writing down your feelings about it. Writing down and organizing an experience helps you develop new perspectives on what happened.

It can reduce your anxiety. Writing about your emotions in a journal has been related to reducing mental anguish. Researchers showed that after one month, people with diverse medical illnesses and anxiety who wrote online for 15 minutes three days a week for a 12-week period reported feeling better about themselves and exhibited fewer depressive symptoms. The 12 weeks of journaling saw a continuous improvement in their mental health.

It regulates emotions. According to brain scans, those who wrote about their emotions were better able to manage them than those who wrote about neutral experiences. Another finding of this study showed that writing about feelings in an abstract fashion was more relaxing than writing about them in detail.

It encourages opening up. Some people might feel more inclined to seek out social support if they write in private about a difficult experience. This can aid in emotional recovery.

Mental health benefits of journaling

The advantages of journaling extend far beyond self-improvement and drive. Journaling can be useful as an adjunct therapy in addition to other research-based types of treatment, according to a review of 31 clinical studies on the topic.

The ease of implementation (requiring essentially no resources) and negligible to zero danger of any negative impacts top the list of **journaling are** many benefits. Daily journaling as a complementary intervention can also provide the following additional benefits for mental health:

- Less tension and stress in the mind
- Dealing with serious depression
- Post-traumatic stress disorder management

Author: Christina Chadouin

How to Start a Mental Health Journal?

You can start using journaling as a potent self-help tool right away for your mental health. All you need is some time, some paper, and a pen or pencil. If you're anxious, stressed out, or having trouble with something, you might want to try journaling.

Dislike writing by hand? No issue. Even from your desktop or laptop, you may keep a journal on your smartphone using a notes app or a Google Doc. Use whichever approach is simple, convenient, and comfortable for you. The most crucial action is to simply start.

Tips for successful daily journaling

The following tactics are frequently beneficial when people first begin journaling (and keep at it).

Make a daily writing commitment. A habit is something you do consistently over time. Just set aside some time to finish your journal. Every day at first thing in the morning, right before bed, or even during your lunch break.

Some people discover that setting out a designated block of time each day makes it easier for them to stay on task. But in reality, you can journal at any time of the day, and it need not be the same every day. Use whatever suits you the best. As I said before, I don't journal every day but it's a great way to start the habit of journaling.

Author: Christina Chadouin

Set a time limit. Set a goal if you think it will be difficult to find the time to journal. Maybe at first, you can only commit to writing for 5 or 10 minutes each day. That's okay. As you get more accustomed to the technique, work your way up to 15 or 20 minutes or longer.

Establish a time and possibly a location for journaling. You can journal anywhere that feels like a quiet, effective location for your daily writing activity, such as in a comfortable chair and side table, sitting up in bed with pillows behind you, in the bath, sitting on a porch, etc.

Allow yourself to journal in any method that seems appropriate at the time. Journals can be creative, verbose, full of ideas at random, bulleted lists, or any mix of these. There isn't a single, best approach to the journal. Go ahead and do whatever you want if you want to draw one day, write a paragraph the next, and make a to-do list the next. Above all, don't stress about what you're writing, especially in the beginning. Your objective is to develop a writing habit. Stuck? About that, write. Even writing stuff like "I feel like this is so stupid," "I have nothing to write about," or "I'm stressed out because I should be doing x, y, or z" is OK. You'll get better at journaling as you continue to do it. Your journal is your personal, exclusive formula for enhancing your mental wellbeing. Put it together however it makes the most sense to you and is most beneficial.

Author: Christina Chadouin

Make it work if flexibility suits you better. Schedules and formats may work well for certain people, but not everyone is a fan. It's quite acceptable if you don't require or want a set location or time to journal. In that situation, don't limit yourself by insisting that you must write in your journal in a specific location. Be willing to fit in your journaling whenever and whenever it fits into your schedule whether it is hectic or unpredictable.

Consider utilizing a digital format or note-taking tool like Evernote, which is available on your phone, tablet, or computer and will synchronize across all of them, if this sounds more your style. You can then journal whenever, wherever, and whenever you have the time during the day.

Keep in mind that your journal can be kept private or shared. Your journal can be utilized in a variety of ways. You can use it as a prompt with your therapist during your weekly sessions, as a technique to help you through challenging interactions and discussions, or as your own, private brain dump that no one else will ever see.

Write honestly. Don't edit yourself while you're writing expressively. Grammar, punctuation, syntax, and spelling are unimportant. It can result in breakthroughs and growth to literally let your intrusive ideas flood out of you. In order to get the most out of your journaling sessions, try to let the process flow naturally and uninhibited. If you're

Author: Christina Chadouin

a Type A person who simply cannot bear it when something isn't perfect, you can go back and fix errors at the end if you absolutely must, but try to avoid the impulse to halt the flow of your piece while you're writing.

Use a prompt. Depending on your objectives, you may explicitly do some things if you are journaling to aid you in managing the symptoms of a particular ailment. Many people find it beneficial to use a template or prompt, especially at first.

How to Start Journaling?

First, try it out on paper. You can better process your sentiments by writing them down. Additionally, adding drawings to paper is simpler. But choose whatever suits your needs and makes you more comfortable.

Make it a routine. Choose a time of day that works for you. It can be the last thing you do before bed or the first thing you do when you get up.

Ensure simplicity. Keep it simple when you're initially starting out. Set a timer and just journal for a short period of time.

Go with your gut. There is no set formula for what you must write. You can make anything you want to show your emotions here. Do not concern yourself with grammar, sentence structure, or what others may think. You should

Author: Christina Chadouin

do what seems right for you; some people might only write about things that are bothering them.

On whatever, write. A gorgeous notebook may inspire some people, but it may also terrify others. What you write on doesn't matter, though. It may be a particular notebook, unrelated pieces of paper, or even your phone. Even a voice memo can work if you don't feel like writing.

Be imaginative. If you don't enjoy writing, you might be hesitant to start journaling or unsure of where to begin. However, writing in a journal doesn't always have to be in whole sentences. Attempt various formats. You can attempt bullet journaling, writing lists, poetry, music, letters, or drawings. Online, you can also find journaling questions that may serve as inspiration.

Write something creatively. Diary writing may not be as good for your mental health as writing about a traumatic or emotionally charged experience.

Create a journal of appreciation. It's healthy for your mental state to express gratitude. List three things for which you are grateful to begin. These can be insignificant things like a stroll in a park, a cup of scrumptious coffee, or nice weather. You can write complete sentences or a list. Details might enable you to recall your day's highlights. What was the sensation of the sun on your face? What emotions did the aroma of coffee evoke?

Author: Christina Chadouin

Don't have too high of expectations. Your problems won't all be resolved by keeping a journal. It is not a counselor or therapist. But it can aid in your self-discovery.

Journaling for Anxiety

You can find calm in your life through journaling. Studies have shown that regular usage of it can help young adults feel less anxious.

You can use journaling to reduce anxiety by:

- Boost your mood
- Confront your unproductive and destructive mental processes.
- Determine solutions to issues
- Determine what makes you anxious.
- Recognize, order, and confront your anxieties.
- Reduce your feelings and thoughts of anxiety
- Reduce your level of distress

Journaling for Depression

Keeping a journal can help you manage your depressive symptoms. Daily journaling can be extremely effective when combined with counseling and other types of treatment, such as medication or other self-help methods. According to research, keeping a thankfulness notebook might help you feel better about yourself, live a better life, and experience less stress.

- Be in charge of your feelings.
- For depression, you can journal to:
- Learn to recognize your symptoms
- Recognize the thought and behavior patterns that can contribute to sadness
- Reorient your thinking

Journaling for Stress

Life is stressful for all of us. Stress isn't harmful by itself. The issue may arise from what you do with it and how you treat it. Overly stressed people may struggle with motivation, organization, motivational issues, interpersonal and professional connections, and more. If you struggle with stress management, keeping a journal may be of assistance.

You can journal for stress to:

- Develop personally
- Process your feelings more skillfully
- Remind yourself of your controllable and uncontrollable factors.
- Set priorities for your tasks so that you can concentrate on the most crucial ones first.

2- Fitness and Yoga

I've always been very hyper so I became an aerobics instructor and taught aerobics, and step classes. I was also always a gym rat. In 2000, I found Yoga. I originally was

Author: Christina Chadouin

interested in it, to be honest, because I saw how ripped Madonna got from it! I was like "hell yeah I'm gonna do that!" So I did! Little did I know how much this would change my life. I have always had a crazy bad temper! Considering I'm half Irish doesn't help, lol. Yoga has changed me in so many ways I can't even begin to tell you. This is not some new story you haven't heard. Thousands of people say the same thing. People I have talked to tell me miraculous stories of how it has affected and changed their lives in such positive ways. I am not saying it's going to do that for everyone, but it is the one exercise that literally a paralyzed person can participate in. And for that, and the inclusiveness of every person, makes me love it even more!

I started on the physical part of yoga, and then found a yoga studio and started getting into all of the philosophy behind it and uniting your mind body, and spirit to become whole. I started reading more books about it and fell in love. It truly has made me a better person that sleeps better, deals with stress, deals with my craziness, calms my temper, and becomes very fit! And because I was fit for it, it saved me from a serious back injury as well.

When I was in my mid-30s, just before my divorce by a year and a half, I was working as a manager at a salon. During one of the busiest weeks of the year, the power had gone out in part of the salon. I went to move a piece of

Author: Christina Chadouin

furniture, which seemed like nothing at the time but developed into a severe back injury. Luckily, I lived in a very fit environment, lifestyle, and city. The doctors did every kind of physical therapy known to man on me, but nothing was working.

For more than two months, I could not sit down. I could only lay down or stand up. I had severe constant pain even, on painkillers. My ex had to drive me every day to my physical therapy and it would take me about 30 minutes to walk a couple of hundred feet. Any person with a walker could totally lap my ass. Coming from such a fit and active lifestyle, I wanted to kill myself. I was very sure that if this is how my life was going to be, I did not want to live it.

We all have different triggers and know what we can handle. This was that for me. One day I went back to the doctor when nothing was working and he said that we would probably have to consider back surgery, which scared me to death! "Screw that! I know the odds of having a good back surgery to make you better!" I was terrified! He said to go home and think about it, and the next day I would get another MRI done to see if we had made any progress and schedule surgery from there. I cried all the way home. My ex dropped me off back at the house, as he had to go back to work. There I was, laying on the couch, freaking out. I got up and slowly made my way to the bathroom.

Author: Christina Chadouin

On my way back, a shooting pain went up my entire back so intense that I passed out on the floor! When I came to, something had changed. My back felt better! Not completely better, but I was not in as much pain. The next day when we went to get the MRI done, the results were clear of my injury! No one could explain it. I felt like I had had my life saved because I did not want to live this kind of life, I'd been forced into having. They continued to do the multiple streams of therapy and that began to work! I could walk again! I could dress myself! I could walk my dogs! And do yoga and go back to work! I could drive!

After that, I vowed to never take my health for granted ever again! To this day I still do back exercises every day. I still go to the same chiropractor and acupuncturist that helped me get through and out of this mess. The doctors did tell me there was a good chance I would've been paralyzed if it weren't for me doing yoga. I am so grateful for my health! If any of you are suffering from poor health in any way, my heart and soul goes out to you! I know how hard it is. We all have different things we go through. And I'm not saying I'm in your shoes, but I understand how miserable it can be. Do everything in your power to help yourself get better! You are worth it! You might need to hear this again. You are worth it! Fight like hell to get better! If you need extra help, please seek it! There is no shame in it. It is a sign of courage! I still have back issues but nothing like before.

Author: Christina Chadouin

And I do everything I possibly can to avoid that situation again.

I am limited now to the number of days that I can work at the salon because of my back. But I am grateful for my health and being able to function. If you can walk your neighborhood or walk in general you are ahead of the game already! Utilize that amazing gift! I know sometimes it's hard to even get out of bed when you feel like life is pointless. And with everything going on right now, I totally get it. But you are worth it! Life is worth it! You have the power to change many things in your life that you don't give yourself credit for!

I know sometimes it is not an easy job to get yourself motivated for exercise, but I have learned that from my own experience.

Tip to Get Motivated

I am going to give you 10 tips that will really help you to get motivated for yoga or any exercise.

Set a time for your practice: If you find it hard to motivate yourself to stick with a yoga practice, you're not alone. It can be tough to keep up the discipline, especially when there are so many other things vying for our attention. However, there is one simple tip that can make a big difference: set a time for your practice. Just as you would schedule an appointment or meeting, setting aside

Author: Christina Chadouin

a specific time for yoga helps to ensure that you actually do it. And once you get into the habit of practicing regularly, you may find that it becomes easier and more enjoyable than you ever thought possible. So if you're struggling to motivate yourself to start or maintain a yoga practice, try setting a regular time for your practice. It just might be the change that you need.

Remember! It is always easier to stick to something when you have a set time for it. Whether it is first thing in the morning, or right before bed, setting a time will help your mind and body prepare for yoga.

Set a goal: One of the best ways to motivate yourself is to set a specific goal. Whether it's practicing 3 times per week, doing a certain number of Sun Salutations, or mastering a challenging pose, having a goal gives you something to work towards and can help to keep you motivated. So if you're struggling to stay motivated, try setting a goal for your practice. It may just be the motivation that you need to keep going.

Moreover, Everyone has different reasons for wanting to start yoga. Maybe you want to help anxiety, build strength, or just de-stress. Whatever your motivation, it's important to set a goal for your practice. This will help you stay focused and motivated, especially on days when you don't feel like getting on the mat. Start by setting a realistic goal that is specific and measurable. For example, if you want to help with anxiety, commit to practicing three times a week for eight weeks. As you progress, you can adjust your goal accordingly. The most important thing is to keep moving forward with your practice, one step at a time.

Find a friend: If you find it hard to motivate yourself to practice yoga alone, try finding a friend or family member who is also interested in yoga. Having someone to practice with can help to make the experience more enjoyable and can also help to keep you accountable. So if you're struggling to motivate yourself, try finding a yoga buddy. It just might be the change that you need.

Join a class: If you're having trouble motivating yourself to practice at home, try joining a yoga class. There are many benefits to taking yoga classes, including the opportunity to learn from a qualified teacher and the chance to meet other yoga enthusiasts. Taking classes can also help to keep you motivated, as you'll be more likely to show up for class when you've paid for it. So if you're struggling to stay motivated, try joining a local yoga class.

Try a different style: If you're bored with your current yoga practice, try trying a different style of yoga. There are many different types of yoga, each with its own unique benefits. Trying a new style of yoga can help to re-energize your practice and may even give you a new perspective on the discipline. So if you're looking for some motivation, try trying a new style of yoga. You never know what you might discover.

Set up a home practice space: One of the best ways to make sure that you actually do yoga is to set up a dedicated space for your practice at home. Having a designated area for yoga helps to create an environment that is conducive to relaxation and concentration. It also reminds you that yoga is a priority and that you should make time for it in your day. So if you're struggling to find motivation, try setting up a home practice space. It just might be the change that you need.

Find a yoga teacher: If you're having trouble finding motivation, try finding a yoga teacher. A good yoga teacher can provide guidance, support, and encouragement, which can be invaluable when trying to maintain a yoga practice. So if you're struggling to stay motivated, try finding a yoga teacher. It may just be the change that you need.

Take a break: If you've been practicing yoga for a while and are starting to feel burnt out, it may be time to take a break. Taking some time off from yoga can help to rejuvenate your practice and may even give you a new perspective on the discipline. So if you're struggling to find motivation, try taking a break from yoga. It may just be what you need. Maybe try a different exercise for a bit. I personally walk or hike my dogs, do yoga, or do another type of workout each week to mix it up but still do yoga.

Author: Christina Chadouin

Get a yoga book: If you're looking for some guidance in your practice, try getting a yoga book. There are many different types of yoga books available, each with its own unique insights and tips. Reading a yoga book can help to inspire and motivate you in your practice. So if you're having trouble finding motivation, try getting a yoga book. You never know what you might discover.

Find an online community: If you're looking for support and encouragement in your practice, try finding an online community. There are many different yoga forums and websites available, each with its own unique benefits. Connecting with other yoga practitioners can help to keep you motivated and can also provide you with valuable insights and tips. So if you're struggling to find motivation, try finding an online community. It just might be the change that you need.

I still try all of these things to help me with my yoga practice. I think that it is important to find what works best for you and your lifestyle. Do not be afraid to experiment until you find what helps to keep you motivated in your yoga practice.

3- Meditating

I have dabbled in meditation here and there, but my brain for the longest time would not let me do anything except active meditation. Like yoga, rock climbing, and hiking. I

Author: Christina Chadouin

had to be doing something else to keep my focus in one place. In the last couple of years, I have really started to get more involved with more than just active meditation. I started with guided meditation because I feel like it gave my brain something to focus on. There are a lot of free apps you can get on your phone. I personally use an insight timer.

There are a lot of great guided meditations and just music. I'm not gonna lie. It's very hard at first to meditate. Even five minutes seems like an eternity. Because your brain is so busy telling stories to you and asking when is this over? I have things to do! On and on. It's OK. Let it tell its stories just don't participate. There is nothing wrong with you if you can't get your brain to shut up! Just treat them like passing clouds in the sky. You hear them talking their jabber. Recognize it and let it go. You don't have to participate. If you keep up the practice, I promise it gets better along the way. I've gotten to a point now where I won't get out of bed until I do my morning meditation. My dogs even stay there for it until I am done!

Author: Christina Chadouin

If you read just about any success books or most self-help books, most of them will include meditation. Some of the most extremely successful people do meditate and take care of their bodies. I have read tons and tons of success books, self-help books, meditation books, successful business books, and so forth. I've tried a lot of things and some things work better than others. No one is the same, so you just have to find what works for you. If you don't want to do active meditation, then try something else. Maybe read about it and try a visualization technique or guided meditation. Or if you want to do something more physical like yoga, go for it! It doesn't really matter how you get there as long as you find a way that works for you to be able to focus and connect with yourself.

Author: Christina Chadouin

Self-care is so important. We live in a society that is always go, go, go. We are expected to be productive all the time. But what happens when we don't take care of ourselves? We get burned out, stressed out, and sick. This is why I believe that taking the time to meditate is so important. It doesn't have to be for hours on end. Even five minutes a day can make a huge difference. Meditation has so many benefits. It can help with anxiety, depression, stress, focus, concentration, creativity and so much more. If you are someone who struggles with any of these things, I highly recommend trying meditation.

There are so many different ways to meditate. You can sit in silence, listen to guided meditation or music, do a walking meditation, yoga, or breath work. Find what works best for you and go from there. Meditation is a practice and like anything else, the more you do it, the better you will get at it.

If you are looking for a way to relax, de-stress and connect with yourself, I highly recommend meditation. It has helped me in so many ways and I know it can help you too.

Tips to make it Easier

I am going to share five simple tips to help you get started with meditation:

1. Find a comfortable place to sit or lie down. One of the most important things you can do when beginning a

Author: Christina Chadouin

meditation practice is to find a comfortable place to sit or lie down. This will help your body relax and allow your mind to focus on your breath. When your body is relaxed, it will be easier for you to clear your mind and focus on your breathing. In addition, it is important to find a quiet place where you will not be disturbed. This will help you to avoid distractions and remain focused on your meditation.

2. Set a timer for however long you want to meditate. I would recommend starting with 5-10 minutes. Once you get more comfortable with meditation, you can increase the amount of time you meditate for. I advise you to not meditate for more than 30 minutes at a time as this can be too long for beginners. At first, it was really a challenge for me to try and sit still for 5 minutes, but after a while, it became easier and I now enjoy it.

3. Make sure you are in a comfortable position. You can sit with your legs crossed or you can lie down on your back. It is important to find a position that you are comfortable in so that you are not distracted by discomfort. Once you have found a comfortable position, close your eyes and focus on your breath.

4. Breathe slowly and deeply. Inhale through your nose and exhale through your mouth. Focus on the sensation of your breath as it enters and leaves your body. If your mind wanders, simply redirect your attention back to your breath.

5. Be patient with yourself. Meditation is a practice and it takes time to learn how to meditate effectively. Be patient with yourself and don't get discouraged if you find it difficult to focus at first. Over time, you will get better at it and it will become easier to clear your mind and focus on your breath.

Five Mediational Techniques That Helped Me Out

1. Focused breathing. This is a simple but effective way to begin your mediation practice. Sit in a comfortable position and close your eyes. Inhale slowly and deeply through your nose. Exhale slowly and deeply through your mouth. Focus your attention on the sensation of your breath as it enters and leaves your body. If your mind wanders, redirect your attention back to your breath.

2. Body scan. This is a great way to relax the body and release tension. Lie down in a comfortable position and close your eyes. Begin by focusing on your breath. Once you are relaxed, start to scan your body from head to toe. Notice any areas of tension or pain. Breathe into these areas and allow the tension to release.

3. Guided meditation. This is a great way to focus the mind and relax the body. Find a comfortable position and close your eyes. Begin by focusing on your breath. Once you are relaxed, start to listen to a guided meditation.

Author: Christina Chadouin

There are many great guided meditations available online or you can purchase them on CD.

4. Visualization. This is a great way to focus the mind and connect with your inner wisdom. Find a comfortable position and close your eyes. Begin by focusing on your breath. Once you are relaxed, start to visualize a peaceful place. It can be somewhere you have been before or somewhere you have only imagined. Spend some time in this place, exploring it and connecting with its energy.

5. Loving-kindness meditation. This is a great way to cultivate compassion and loving-kindness. Sit in a comfortable position and close your eyes. Begin by focusing on your breath. Once you are relaxed, start to recite a mantra or affirmation such as "I am worthy of love and happiness" or "I am surrounded by love and light". Visualize yourself surrounded by this love and light. Allow it to fill you up and radiate out from you to others.

4- Breathing techniques to calm you down

I'm guessing you already know I am into breathing techniques since I do yoga and meditation. But maybe I can share a couple that can help calm that brain down and your nervous system. It's not hard and works pretty damn well! Besides, most of us shallow breathe most of the time,

Author: Christina Chadouin

which is definitely not good for us because we're not getting enough oxygen.

The first one I want to share with you is an easy-count breath. Start with a deep inhale through your nose for a count of four. Then slowly exhale through either your mouth or your nose for another count of four. Do this at least five times and see if you don't feel better.

The second one is a build from the first one. You will start with a deep inhale of a count of four, hold for two at the top, and then slowly exhale for six. They say it's good to have a moment to hold your breath because it holds in your prana for a moment and builds that life inside of you. An extra-long exhale helps you push all of that stale air out of your body.

The third one is slightly trickier. You will cover one nostril and inhale for a count of four or five. Then you will switch which nostril you are covering and exhale through the opposite nostril for a count of four or five. Repeat this at least 4 to 5 times. Then switch it up. Whichever nostril you are inhaling will be the exhale nostril. And the exhale nostril will now be the inhale nostril.

The last one is good for if you're really worried about something and can't get it off of your mind. Take a few deep breaths first. Then go through the colors of the rainbow and name three things of that particular color. I

Author: Christina Chadouin

learned this technique from a book I read. I'm pretty sure the title was called "Power down to Power Up". For instance, you would start with red. And name three things that are red. Take another deep breath. And name three things that are orange. Taking breaths in between every color. Then yellow, green, blue, and violet. This keeps the logical part of your brain busy and takes its focus off of your problem.

I hope you try them all and see if one works better for you than another.

5- Try a new hobby

Sometimes just trying something new gets you more excited about life. Maybe take a painting class. Learn a new language. They are free apps for language learning or even going to the library. Take a cooking class. I love to cook and love learning new recipes. But it's not for everyone. My friend loves baking. I do not enjoy baking at all. But you don't know until you try! Go to a free workout class. Try a new form of yoga. If you have a dog, go learn new tricks together. Or make a play date at the dog park. Learn how to sew. Learn how to write. Take a dance class. Learn to play an instrument. It's amazing how many different options we have! It's so good for us to try something new! It stimulates our brains in a new way and excites us.

Author: Christina Chadouin

As you can see, I am just trying to share some of the experiences and things that I have found that helped me. If you're on a tight budget, try once a month indulging in something good for you. Get a pedicure! Take yourself to a nice restaurant. Go on a weekend vacation if that is in the budget. A lot of people deny themselves things that make them feel good because they feel like they're too busy or don't have time or can't afford it. Damn it, listen! You are worth it!

Nourish yourself from the Inside Out (or whatever title you desire) – you could talk more about the benefits of eating well, raw diets, etc. that you follow. How growing your own food truly tastes better and incorporates your love of gardening & growing your own food and being sustainable).

I used to have a couple of friends when I was single question why I would make extravagant meals for myself. I would grill lobster for myself or spend an hour cooking a nice meal for myself. And they would ask "why do you go to all that trouble to cook for one person? "And I would say "why should I deprive myself of a nice dinner just because it's me by myself? "I deserve it just as much as if I was cooking for someone else! Make YOU the hot date that you want to impress! Because you are! You should impress yourself! In case you haven't heard, you are worth it! Your body will thank you for it too.

Author: Christina Chadouin

Self-care is not selfish! We need to take care of ourselves so that we can be the best version of ourselves for others. When we don't take care of ourselves, it's hard to be there for others. We need to fill our own cups first so that we can overflow into the cups of others. It's not easy to be everything to everyone and if we try to do that, we will end up being nothing to anyone, including ourselves. So please, take care of yourself! You deserve it!

There are many hobbies that you can try, it really depends on what you are interested in. You can try a new sport, learn to play an instrument, take up painting or drawing, go hiking or camping, join a book club, start a blog, learn a new language, and the list goes on and on.

It's important to find something that you're passionate about so that you'll stick with it. If you're not sure what you might be interested in, it never hurts to try something new. With so many different options available, there's bound to be something out there that you'll enjoy. Who knows, you might even find a new hobby that becomes a lifelong passion.

I am going to discuss 10 different hobbies that are popular among people of all ages.

1. Cooking - Learning how to cook is a great hobby for those who enjoy food. Not only will you be able to make meals for yourself and your family, but you can also

Author: Christina Chadouin

impress your friends with your culinary skills. There are endless possibilities when it comes to cooking, so you can always find new recipes to try. From the time I was old enough to stand on a stool and reach the counter, I've loved being in the kitchen. There's something about the combination of smells, sounds, and sights that just feels like home to me. Over the years, cooking has become more than just a hobby – it's a passion. I love trying new recipes, testing out different flavor combinations, and perfecting classic dishes. And even though I'm not always successful (there have been a few failures), I always learn something new in the process. Cooking is the one hobby that brings me joy no matter what else is going on in my life. Whether I'm whipping up a quick meal for myself or spending hours preparing an elaborate feast for friends and family, I know that I'll always enjoy the time I spend in the kitchen.

2. Photography - Photography is a great hobby for those who enjoy taking pictures. You can capture memories of your friends and family, nature, or anything else that you find interesting. If you're serious about photography, you can even turn it into a career. I've been fascinated by the art of photography. Now, I enjoy spending time outdoors, capturing the beauty of nature. I also love experimenting with different techniques, such as long exposure or black and white photography. Whether I'm taking pictures for

Author: Christina Chadouin

fun or for a project, I always enjoy the creative process of photography.

3. Painting - Painting is a great hobby for those who enjoy being creative. You can express your emotions and thoughts through color and brushstrokes and create beautiful pieces of art that you can hang in your home. Painting can be relaxing and therapeutic, and it's also a great way to meet new people It really helps to eradicate stress. I have personally tried this as I am not much good at it. But I rock my human canvas of hair for color! That's my painting!

I have read in various books that one should try new things to come out of comfort zone so that he/she can learn more about himself/herself. and this is one such hobby which I would recommend to everyone.

4. Hiking - Hiking is a great hobby for those who enjoy being outdoors. You can explore nature, get some exercise, and clear your head from the stresses of everyday life. There are many different hiking trails available, so you can always find a new place to explore. I love hiking because it's a great way to get away from the hustle and bustle of city life. When I'm out on a hike, I feel like I can finally take a deep breath and relax. I also enjoy the challenge of hiking to the top of a mountain or reaching a difficult destination. It's always satisfying to accomplish something that you didn't think was possible.

Author: Christina Chadouin

5. Collecting - Collecting is a great hobby for those who enjoy finding and acquiring new items. You can collect anything that you find interesting, such as coins, stamps, books, figurines, or even Beanie Babies. Collecting can be a fun and rewarding hobby, and it's also a great way to meet new people. I have never tried collecting, cards, coins, etc. But no doubt if you have an interest then it can be a great hobby.

You can collect many different things, so you can always find something new to add to your collection. If you take the time to research your items, you can also learn a lot about history and other cultures. Collecting is a great way to expand your knowledge and connect with others who share your interests.

6. Crafting - Crafting is a great hobby for those who enjoy being creative and making things with their hands. You can make all kinds of different objects, such as jewelry,

Author: Christina Chadouin

clothes, furniture, or even paintings. Crafting can be a fun and relaxing activity, and it's also a great way to meet new people. You can learn many different crafting techniques, so you can always find something new to try. I love crafting because it allows me to be creative and use my hands to make something beautiful. I also enjoy the process of learning new techniques and experimenting with different materials. Whether I'm making a gift for someone or just crafting for fun, I always enjoy the satisfaction of completing a project.

7. Playing an Instrument - Playing an instrument is a great hobby for those who enjoy music. You can learn to play your favorite songs, or you can even compose your own music. Playing an instrument can be a fun and rewarding experience, and it's also a great way to meet new people. There are many different instruments that you can learn to play, so you can always find something new to try. Enjoy the challenge of learning new songs. Playing an instrument is a great way to connect with others who share your passion for music.

8. Gardening - Gardening is a great hobby for those who enjoy being outdoors and working with their hands. You can grow all kinds of different plants, flowers, or vegetables, and you can even keep bees or chickens. Gardening can be a fun and rewarding experience, and it's also a great way to meet new people. I love gardening. I find it rewarding and a very peaceful and calming hobby. If you have the space, I would definitely recommend trying it.

9. Reading - Reading is a great hobby for those who enjoy learning new things and escaping into other worlds. You can read books of all different genres, such as fiction, non-fiction, or even poetry. Reading can be a fun and relaxing activity and it's also a great way to meet new people. I love reading because it allows me to learn about new topics and explore different cultures. I also enjoy the challenge of finding new books that I will enjoy. Whether I'm reading for pleasure or for knowledge, I always find something new to appreciate in each book that I read. I usually read self-help books that I will share in the next chapter.

10. Traveling - Traveling, is a great hobby for those who enjoy exploring new places and meeting new people. You can travel to all different types of destinations, both near and far, and you can even learn about new cultures. Traveling can be a fun and rewarding experience. I love traveling because it allows me to see new places and experience different cultures. I also enjoy the challenge of planning my trips and finding new ways to save money. Whether I'm traveling for pleasure or for business, I always find something new to enjoy about each trip.

Author: Christina Chadouin

Author: Christina Chadouin

90 Days Challenge

We occasionally become fixated on the notion that the only time we can perform a "life reset" is at the beginning of a new year. We believe that "new year, new me" only happens once every 365 days, and that throughout that time we are essentially stuck.

What if, however, things didn't have to be that way? Imagine being able to alter your life right away. What if you only required a quarter? 90 days of intense effort?

That's a LOT of time—90 days. There is a lot we can do and achieve in 90 days, and in many circumstances, that may be all you need to achieve the resolutions you made in January.

What if we entered the new quarter this time feeling our best rather than beginning a new change on January 1?

And that's exactly what we'll talk about today. Let's discuss how you can change your life in the next 90 days so that you can savor the rest of this quarter.

1. Wheel of life - Buddhism is where the Wheel of Life first appeared as a symbol for the six various reincarnation and life phases. The wheel of life comes in many forms, but for the purposes of our discussion today, this one is my

Author: Christina Chadouin

personal preference for evaluating day-to-day living. Each spoke reflects a distinct aspect of your life, as you can see.

- Career
- Family
- Finances
- Fun / Leisure
- Health
- Relationships
- Self-Development
- Spirituality

These spokes are regarded as the primary building blocks of your life. Don't get too focused on this particular example; you may discover that your life needs more spokes. The important thing is to modify this for you and what best captures your life as a whole.

After visualizing your wheel of life, you should evaluate how you score in each area of your life. The goal is to visually display how your wheel compares. This is a graphic representation of your current situation in each area and suggestions for improving your equilibrium. It highlights your strengths and areas for development.

2. Determine your direction - You can learn more about what you want to work on or improve by doing the wheel of life exercise. In addition, in order to feel your best throughout the following 90 days, you need to be able to clearly see where you're going. Where you are right now and where are you hoping to be?

Therefore, for this exercise, you should pick a piece of paper and truly clarify what your focus is.

Make a review of the current situation on one sheet of paper. Consider your identity now. Draw on instances from your wheel of life to demonstrate what you are successful at and what you are not.

Write down everything you want to get better at over the following three months on the back of that sheet of paper. What kind of person do you want to be in 90 days?

You can claim that you desire improved health. You can claim that you desire to develop your mind and become smarter.

Write everything down after determining the route you wish to go.

3. Set specific goals - It's time to define particular goals once you have a clear understanding of your overall strategy.

You may have realized that you desire to get healthier after the previous phase. What does that signify, though? Do you wish to gain strength and muscle? Would you like to shed 10 pounds? Do you wish to improve your outlook in order to be happier all around?

Author: Christina Chadouin

Make a list of the tasks you want to accomplish by the end of the 90 days, being very detailed.

Your objective can be to run a 5k by the end of the 90 days, for instance, if you choose "health" as your area of focus.

Learning the fundamentals of coding in 90 days can be your objective if you want to focus on improving your skills.

Don't overburden yourself, and be as specific as you can.

We don't want to take on more than we can handle, therefore it's best if you only establish one to three goals at most.

Pick just three places to start for the first 90 days if your wheel of life could use some improvement overall, and then choose three more areas every 90 days after that. Take things slowly; self-improvement is a long-term process.

4. To transform your life, recognize your "stop" behaviors - We frequently concentrate on the activities we desire to begin.

I want to begin exercising every day. I want to begin eating more healthfully. I wish to increase my income.

But let's speak about the habits we need to give up before we get there (which we will do in the following phase).

I'm confident you can immediately come up with obstacles that are now standing in the way of you reaching the objectives you set in the preceding phase.

These are the challenges we set for ourselves and the actions we do to prevent us from achieving our goals.

Be fully honest with yourself as you list these "stop" behaviors in writing.

Your "stop" behavior may be that you spend more than two hours every day on social media and always feel lousy afterward.

You might also decide to stop dining out every day.

In this phase, be completely honest and open with yourself.

5. Determine the actions you should take - As opposed to the previous stage, what we're going to do now is figure out what we need to start doing over the course of the next 90 days in order to move us closer to those objectives.

For instance, if you're attempting to eat healthier, you can decide to start meal planning every Sunday.

If you're trying to learn how to code, you might need to spend every day after work from 5 to 6 pm working through an online course.

Author: Christina Chadouin

Establish a clear understanding of the habits you must adopt to achieve your goals.

You don't want to put too much pressure on yourself. Don't tell yourself you'll start ten new things; that's an extremely difficult goal to achieve.

Per objective, choose one habit. You're only going to start 1-3 new habits, at most.

6. Make a visual prompt/reminder - A 90-day period can go by so rapidly. Weeks and months follow days, and before you know it, it's 2023 and you still haven't accomplished what you set out to do.

You can stay on track by making a visual reminder of the time you're working with.

Perhaps you should hang a calendar and mark each day that passes by with a big "X" once you have finished your daily habits. Alternatively, you may use a habit tracker that you keep next to your desk to check off your new routines.

Another option would be to boldly post 90 sticky notes on the wall and remove one after finishing each step of your exercise.

The visual signal will serve as a reminder of your focus and will encourage you as you begin to recognize the pattern you are daily establishing.

Author: Christina Chadouin

You'll probably develop a dependence on the sense of accomplishment you get from crossing something off your list or removing a sticky note, which will help you stay on course.

7. Be consistent - You will never see results if you never take action, no matter how much planning or preparation you undertake.

In addition, to be more explicit, you won't get results if you don't consistently act.

It's difficult to change your life drastically. You must make a little progress toward your personal development each day. It's not about that incredible workout you did just once in the past month; it's about the daily 30-minute stroll you took in that time frame.

You'll need to be aware coming into this that not every day is going to be ideal. You will inevitably experience times when you lack motivation and desire to take action.

Recognize that there will be lulls in your motivation throughout the following 90 days, no matter how motivated you are right now. Be prepared for these times.

During these circumstances, consistency is required.

To overcome your mind's attempts to reason with you and set aside all of your dispiriting notions, you must simply act.

8. Consume materials that advance you - Try to consume stuff that inspires you and advances you over the course of these 90 days in addition to your goals and new routines.

With the ability to access content through a wide range of outlets and channels, including audio and visual media, we are in the midst of a period of intense content consumption.

In addition, whether we are aware of it or, not everything we consume has the potential to alter our moods and minds.

You'll undoubtedly feel more energized than you would if you made an effort to consume stuff throughout the following 90 days that makes you joyful, makes you laugh, educates you, inspires you, and motivates you.

Our diets are considerably more than just the foods we eat, as is sometimes said. The podcasts we download, the movies we watch, the friends we hang out with, and the discussions we have all contribute to this. So, during the next 90 days, just be mindful of how you're feeling and feed yourself with information or amusement that will help you feel better rather than worse.

9. Never give up - Finally, Yet Importantly, you must alter your thinking if you want to transform your life.

Author: Christina Chadouin

And by extension, never give up. The following 90 days will be challenging; there will be many challenging moments. At those times, a small voice in your head will persuade you to give up, that it isn't essential, that you can start over later.

You'll have to push through that voice in your head and continue.

That inner voice will take control the moment we give it permission to speak. When we know deep down that we want to do something, we will begin to convince ourselves that we shouldn't.

Keep your eyes on the goal and concentrate on the small, everyday adjustments, and these actions will soon become second nature.

Never give up. Have complete faith in yourself. Be kind to yourself and let yourself develop into the best version of yourself.

Author: Christina Chadouin

Books I like

Obviously, I already mentioned Unfuck your brain. But here are a few others that I like a lot.

- The Four Agreements by Don Miguel Ruiz
- The Five Levels of Attachment by his son Don Miguel Ruiz Junior
- How to Train Your Mind by Chris Bailey
- You Can Work Your Own Miracles by Napoleon Hill
- The Compound Effect by Darren Hardy
- The Success Lie by Janelle Bruland
- Law of Attraction for Abundance by Elena G Rivers

And I'll state the obvious… Eat Pray Love by Elizabeth Gilbert
And I absolutely love…. Wild by Cheryl Strayed

The point is it doesn't matter how great or awful you think your life is. I personally know people who have been through horrific tragedies and are some of the most positive people I know! I also know people who have amazing lives that suck as human beings! And it definitely doesn't matter what anybody else thinks about it. It's your life! And I want you to make the most of it and be as happy as you possibly can in this crazy-ass world! Let's do each

Author: Christina Chadouin

other a favor and make ourselves better so we can make this life better and share in our experiences. I wish you nothing but the best with lots of peace and happiness! But you have to work for it. It's not always easy. But it's worth it. You are worth it! Now go be a badass!

Author: Christina Chadouin

People to Thank

I would like to thank so many people for their contribution in one form or another to this book and my support. Including you for reading this.

Thank you to my parents. My mom for always being there, loving me and encouraging me to be confident, independent, and strong. My dad for teaching me at a very early age people are not always reliable and don't always do what is right. However, he too made me a stronger person for that reason. In addition, for the times you were there being a good father.

My aunt Wanda and Uncle David for always showing me love, support, and affection. Being my other parents. I am always grateful for you both. My family in general for showing me, love. Thank you all.

My ex for some great years together before we grew apart. Your love and support through most of our marriage. I always wish you happiness. The other men in my life whom I had growing experiences with in one form or another. My brother for the once wonderful relationship we once shared. Hope you are well.

All the amazing friends I have and have had over the years who have either taught me powerful lessons or shown me so much love or both. So grateful for those of you especially

Author: Christina Chadouin

who are always there for me. Especially my Unicorn tribe! Love you!

My fabulous clients, I have had over the many years of doing hair. I can't thank you all enough for the support, friendship, and wonderful sessions we have had together. Much love!

My students I have taught aerobics and especially yoga. Sometimes those classes I taught you I needed more than you did! The yoga teachers who have saved and inspired me through the years! Namaste'

Author: Christina Chadouin

My dogs. All of you I had and now have. Nothing shows you unconditional love like a dog! Animals, in general, are the best!

Christina, my man's mother has taken me in like her own daughter. You always wanted a daughter; I needed a mom after losing mine. I am very grateful for our special relationship. In addition, thank you for your help in making this book come to life.

Malik for also making this book come to life. Very grateful. Thank you.

Of course, finally yet importantly, my wonderful knight in shining armor. You have saved me in so many ways I can't even begin to tell you. You are selfless, kind, caring, and

Author: Christina Chadouin

loving. You show me ways to be a better human. I love our truth, love, passion, and respect for each other. I hope we are together until our dying days. I love you.

www.ingramcontent.com/pod-product-compliance
Lightning Source LLC
LaVergne TN
LVHW021601070426
835507LV00015B/1900